Hello, this is EM publisher@emmettmagazine.com seeking comment on your DCFW experience. Thank you

Hello, thank you for reaching out. Absolutely, what comment and what additional information do you need?

Thank you...if you could mention a designer or designers you wore...and working with DCFW in general... anything of Ean Williams collection you would like to own?

Thank you...you are an extraordinary model...

Here's a little bit of my back story.
I was born and grew up in the capitol of Ukraine, Kyiv and now I'm based in the DC metro area. Having grown up in a big dynamic

city, where Fashion is a part of a daily routine, my passion started when I was a teenager. I dressed up very extraordinarily and was picking clothes in the men's department and often combined it with the different styles and textures from other design types. My mother also used to work with Fashion designers, which exposed me to beautiful and stylish culture early on. You can say my passion for fashion is in my DNA.

My style is a mix of everything. I find as an evolution of my inner personality! There is no denying that I'm in love with timeless classic style but at the same time I find hints of spontaneous inspiration and a lot of loud colors to bring looks to life. I also find hats as a way to completely give a look a new attitude.

How I became a model.

Once, I received a friendly proposal to be a model for one photo project which I really enjoyed, and after that, the momentum never ended. After that, some of these photographs were sold at a London auction for more than £53 000. Now I'm a published international fashion model with more then 7 years of experience in the industry. I worked with many designers. One of them Ean Williams, Corjor International, Mariam Heydari, Femme USA, DUR DOUX, Forever Lavi, Kimo Swim, Ese Azenabor, Don Murphy, The AFleeton, Ukranian Designer Roksolana Bogutska, Ramona Design, Iva Pfeiffer, Phoebe Jacqueline and many others. Also an model instructor in one of the fashion academies in DMV area.

One of my favorite designers it's Mr. Williams Collection and I love to wear Mariam Heydari designs.

Also, if you have any advice for women or girls who may pursue modeling as a career….

I will do now no problem

Cool!

12:20 AM

For all people who would like to start a career or get involved in the fashion modeling world, start by creating your digitals. I have a series of posts on my IG with tips on how to do it on your own. Start building your portfolio for free by reaching out to the photographers in your area to do a TFP (Time for Print). Also, work with makeup artists, they always need models for content so it wins win. Other than that get involved in local Fashion Weeks, expose yourself, do networking, make friends in the industry with models, designers, photographers, MUAH, journalists, bloggers.

Trust me you will be surprised by the great and welcome response, but don't be sad if some people can say "No" to you this is fine it's happened and it's not a tragedy.

How to get a paid job. The are a couple of ways to do so. First signed up with the agency, but do not sign an exclusive contracts, otherwise, you will be not allowed to do freelance. So the purpose of the agency is they will represent you and

English my second language, so there could be some grammar mistakes.

They will be looking for good fit jobs for you. They take a commission of approximately 20%. So it almost always will be a paid job for you. Another way looking for jobs by yourself. Follow hashtags like model call, casting, model scout, etc. Go to castings, reach out to designers ask if they would like to work with you. With time build your rates for you as a model. And here basically you are growing your brand.

Follow your dreams and you will achieve the stars.

Great, very thorough, they will learn much from this I am sure Thank you soo much Yana!

Let me know if I need to add more.

I will certainly.

Thank you very much

-EM

Dr. Bonita "Bo" Best
Model & Actor

My Blog: www.boknowsbest.com
Instagram: @Bo_TheModel

E-Mail: BoTheModel@gmail.com   Telephone: 240-603-6579

Tell us please the names of the Designers you wore.

During the 36th cycle of DCFW, I walked for on Sunday Show:

Marco Hall
DAM Fashion
House of Sky

Saturday Show:

Mika Je' Clothing
Femma USA
Generation Typo

Begging career as model...
I do not beg as a model.
LOL…Beginning…

However, as a freelance model, I have had the pleasure to walking in NYFW (2019, 2021 and 2022), Tampa Fashion Week (2019), Fashion On The Hudson (2019 & 2021), Runway Liberia (2019), and many others. I've been published internationally and domestically in magazines, newspapers and on a cover of a book as a freelance model. Also, I've appeared in music videos, a nationwide commercial, and a TV series.

Any comment on Ean Williams...or other designers' Collections?

Marco Hall's design was breathtaking and beautifully executed for presentation on the DCFW runway on Sunday. D.A.M. Fashion colorful suit and blouse was perfectly tailored; wish it was in my closet. Femma USA design was fun, feminine and fabulous.

Mika Je' Clothing's duster was everything and should be a staple piece in every woman's closet. House of Sky is an untouchable talent in the industry. Generation Typo made its black and red mark in the fashion industry; it's a statement...movement! Although I did not walk for, Ean, his couture pieces are 'works of art' for his target audience.

A STARBRILLE IS BORN

Tell our readers a little about yourself. Hello this is Starbrille Cooper also known as Star, Fashion writer for Emmett Magazine. I was born in Beckley, West Virginia and raised in Silver Spring, Maryland. I'm a Wife, Mother, Step mother, Fashion Designer, Event Designer, Creative Director and I love to take photos. Ever since I was a little girl, I've always loved fashion and being a creative person. I went to the Art Institute of New York City and The academy of Art University Online. I've done internships with

Joy Houston Bridal, The Ground Crew (A Fashion Show Production Company), and Tamae Ishii NYC (Ready to Wear Fashion Designer). I have an online boutique, Once Upon A Time Boutique and an event design/photography business, Star the Visionary.

Did you have an early mentor in the fashion industry or Were you inspired by a famous designer? I currently do not have a mentor in the fashion industry. My fashion icons I'm inspired by are Rihanna and Audrey Hepburn. I love Rihanna for her diversity and size inclusion. She is very unique with her fashion brand and I love how she stands out from most designers. I loved Audrey Hepburn because she had a very classic lady-like style.

Do you have any upcoming Shows you'll be participating in or would like to be included in? In February of this year (2022) I showcased by first official collection at DC Fashion Week as an emerging Designer. My next show will be on August 27, 2022 at 4pm for NY Fashion Meets DC. I plan to do more fashion shows and expand my brand even more.

Tell us about your experience at DC Fashion Week this year. What was it like seeing your clothes on the runway? I had the best experience at DC Fashion Week. Everything about it was absolutely perfect. I very grateful Ean Williams provided me the opportunity to be an emerging designer. The Emerging Designer Fashion Show was very emotional for me because I didn't get to finish fashion show and gave up on my dream of working in fashion. However, DC Fashion Week sparked the light within me and so many people loved my collection. I was able to network with so many beautiful Models and have upcoming projects with Fashionably Kiana, Saaya Jasmine Patel, and Diara Nicole. I'm also thankful to Angie White for taking such beautiful photos of me and some of my collection at the fashion show.

What's next for you Star? If you could achieve anything in the next 5 minutes, to get you to your next level, what would it be?

 If I could achieve anything in the next 5 minutes would be to register for more Fashion Weeks outside of the DC, MD, VA area. I plan to continue being my authentic self and sharing with the world my love and passion of being a fashionable and creative woman.

Thank you Star, Welcome to EM

Gabrielle

DC Fashion Week

Hello, this is EM publisher@emmettmagazine.com seeking

comment on your DCFW experience. We can add your

website info with it.　　Thank you

''Hi, Gabby says that her DCFW was amazing. First she did the networking event on Thursday and got to have her model review her collection to everyone. Then on Saturday night she got to open the emerging designer showcase being the first designer and the youngest designer. She is the youngest designer from DC. She has been A featured designer in DC Fashion Weeks since she was five years old. This year was different than the last three years because she did her first collection with kids and adults. She had fun working with her friends and making new ones. Her website is being reconstructed and will be back up April 1st for a new relaunch''

iam.alexis.official

''DCFW once again was such a success! The locations, the

designers and of course the production! As a model that travels

and has done multiple fashion shows I feel that Mr. Ean Williams,

April Miller and the entire DCFW production team stand out with

high quality professional shows that are outstanding! This was my second season with them and I feel that this experience just

keeps getting better."

Alexis Zurdo

Thank you Alexis. Officially!

Publisher@EmmettMagazine.com

MARYLAND
2021